A Small Book of UNICORNS

Paintings by Jay Burch

Text by Josephine Bradley

POMEGRANATE ARTBOOKS *San Francisco*

Published by Pomegranate Artbooks
Box 6099, Rohnert Park, California 94927

Pomegranate Europe Ltd.
Fullbridge House
Maldon, Essex CM9 7LE, England

Text by Josephine Bradley was first published in *In Pursuit of the Unicorn* (Pomegranate Artbooks, 1980).

Library of Congress Cataloging-in-Publication Data

Burch, Jay
    A small book of unicorns / paintings by Jay Burch ; text by
Josephine Bradley.
       p.   cm.
    ISBN 0-87654-358-1
    1. Unicorns. I. Bradley, Josephine. II. Title.
GR830.U6B87 1995
759.13—dc20   94-49450
                                        CIP

Pomegranate Catalog No. A778

Designed by Peter Howells

Printed in Korea
00 99 98 97 96 95   6 5 4 3 2 1

First Edition

The unicorn has kept its elusive magic and charm through many centuries. Writers, scientists, sculptors, and painters have pursued it relentlessly, but none has been able finally to say: "I've caught it. Here is the unicorn laid out, pinned down, defined, and categorized once and for all." For this we should be thankful since a captive unicorn would take its place irrevocably in the world of facts, like a far distant star newly sighted and named, or the once secret surface of the moon now charted and photographed for all to see.

Why should a beast with a single horn so capture humankind's imagination? Why has the unicorn so outstripped in popularity other mythical creatures: the manticore, the griffin, the mermaid, to name but a few? Only the dragon, rampaging through history from ancient China to twentieth-century children's fantasy, can rank as an equal in legend and popularity.

Unicorn lore is a box of treasures. If we search carefully within, we find creatures to satisfy all the demands of our imagination. Here are maidens and monsters, nightmares and daydreams, tiny fragile animals of gleaming purity, and great charging warriors who scream through forests of chaos and fear. Godlike at one moment, the unicorn is charmed and cajoled, only to be hunted the next for the magical properties of its horn. It grows a tail and plunges through the waves; it stretches out great wings and takes to the skies. It is truly a creature of dreams.

But dreams are real, too, whether they be waking fantasies that accompany us like silent shadows, or fragmented pictures that paint themselves on the dark canvas of our sleep. This reality is the unicorn's terrain. It lives here in whatever guise we give it: a beast of solitude and beauty, a creature of force, wisdom, or calm. Let us hold fast to the essence of the unicorn—and hope that in spirit it will remain forever untamed.

The first unicorns, as such, seem to have appeared in written accounts rather than in pictorial representations. Ctesia, a Greek historian who lived about 400 B.C., describes a one-horned animal rather like an ass. It lives,

he tells his readers, in India. Although Ctesia himself had never been to India, and although it seems that much of what he wrote was speculation and elaboration, his writings were very popular. People were intrigued by the idea of a unicorn and readily accepted its existence. India was sufficiently remote from Greece to harbor an unlimited supply of curious creatures; it was surely not unreasonable that the unicorn should be one of these. Aristotle obviously believed in it, since he propounded a theory about its single horn: its hooves, he reasoned, because they were solid rather than cloven, required an unusually large amount of bone for an animal of this type; hoof and horn being formed of the same material, when it came to making the latter there was only enough left for one.

A later Greek writer, Megasthenes, told of a one-horned animal that he referred to as a unicorn. His report is of a creature known as the cartazoon, about which he learned from Buddhist monks. It appears to have resembled a horse in size, though it had some features of the rhinoceros.

Prior to these Western sources there was apparently a similar beast in China as early as 2500 B.C. This animal, known as Ch'i-lin, was held in great esteem. It lived to the age of 1,000 and possessed a very musical voice quite different from that of its braying European counterpart. "Its cry," says one writer, "was like the sound of bells." Its skin, moreover, could radiate beams of five sacred colors: red, yellow, blue, white, and black. There seems to be some question as to whether the Ch'i-lin had one horn or two, but it was without doubt a legendary beast of considerable standing. We do not know whether its reputation spread to ancient Greece and Rome, but the veneration with which it was treated certainly reminds us of the respect the unicorn acquired at a later period.

Thus in early descriptions of the unicorn's shape and size conflict already arises. The same is true of accounts of its temperament. Was it fierce like the rhinoceros, which was noted for being able to defeat even the elephant in battle and gouge open its stomach with the aid of its horn? Or was it a creature of gentleness and solitude, preferring to wander at will in remote mountain

pastures? Both ideas are put forward by Greek and Roman writers, a signal that even at the time of its introduction into the Western world the unicorn's nature was open to speculation.

Regardless, however, of such contradictions as to the animal's color, size, and disposition, not to mention the actual location of its horn, which seems to have fluctuated between the nose and the forehead, in people's minds the unicorn came to exist as surely as did the rhinoceros, the ibex, and the elephant. All had heard tell of such beasts and had marveled that nature could produce such variations. Few, if any, had seen them. It is for this reason that in the illustrations for twelfth- and thirteenth-century manuscripts we find an inspired mixture of fantasy and reality. Tigers appear spotted instead of striped, elephants' trunks are little bigger than the snouts of pigs, wild goats leap down from mountaintops and support themselves on their horns. Unlike most of these animals, however, the unicorn had one great advantage: it remained a creature of hearsay and speculation. Elephants, tigers, and the like were all ultimately

seen and documented firsthand by numerous travelers. Over the centuries they lost their magical appeal and eventually found their place in zoos and natural history books. The unicorn, conversely, took up permanent residence in the realm of the imagination.

In the meantime, however, it still had many real mountain pastures to graze in, many living adversaries to fight or flee. The Old Testament associates it with both good and evil. "Save me from the lion's mouth: thou hast heard me also from among the horns of unicorns," says Psalm 22, line 21. Here the unicorn is obviously an animal to be feared, named in the same verse as the lion itself, most powerful of all wild animals. Although the Bible does not actually mention the fact, several religious writers suggested that the unicorn was present in the Garden of Eden, where it is frequently depicted with Adam and Eve. In this context it seems to suggest a benign presence comforting man and woman (now clad in fig leaves) after their fall from innocence. Thus we can see that in the Western tradition symbolism and allegory started to play an important part in the concept of the unicorn as soon as it was used in a religious context. From then on the real beast and the allegorical one were intermingled for many centuries. What happened to the unicorn after the Garden of Eden is a matter for conjecture. Perhaps it perished in the flood. Indeed, some folk tales suggest it was too arrogant to board Noah's ark. Others mention that it swam valiantly behind but was drowned as a result of many birds perching on its horn. Such conjectures, however, are of minor importance. For those who needed it later—sculptors, artisans, painters—the unicorn had certainly not perished. It still stood clearly in their imaginations by day and flew through their dreams at night.

When we reach the Middle Ages we find the unicorn at the height of its popularity. This was a time when people were extremely curious about the world around them, and somewhat gullible, too. Travelers' tales were much sought after and could be embroidered at will to satisfy the eager audience since the listeners were hardly likely to set foot outside their own village, let alone cross the boundary of their native country. In conditions such

as these the unicorn flourished, together with countless other marvelous beasts such as griffins, manticores, and hippogriffs. The gullibility of the general public was never so well illustrated as in the case of Sir John Mandeville, whose totally invented "Traveler's Tales" were taken as gospel truth for many years. In these, Mandeville recounted having seen with his own eyes not merely fantastic animals but also numerous travesties of the human species: men without heads but with eyes and mouths in their shoulders, others whose ears hung down to their knees or who ran on hooves as swiftly as horses.

For the people who listened open-mouthed to such stories, the unicorn was simply one more marvel. Early works on "physiology" had wide audiences, and from these writings developed bestiaries, books that described the peculiarities of animals both real and imaginary, using them as religious and moral symbols. Here is an example from *Le bestiare Divin* by Guillaume:

The unicorn represents Jesus Christ, who took on him our nature in the virgin's womb, was

17

betrayed to the Jews, and delivered into the hands of Pontius Pilate. Its one horn signifies the Gospel truth, that Christ is one with the Father.

Allegorical texts such as these were painstakingly illustrated in the rich, glowing style of the monasteries, for the Middle Ages were above all a time of visual imagery. From its cathedrals and monuments peer down at us fantastic creatures whose hooves, tails, and horns speak louder than words to the imagination of the passerby. In the stained glass windows, the tapestries, the carved seats and doorways, stand men and women, dogs and cats, dragons and unicorns, side by side in a world where miracles and monsters were as credible as plagues and floods.

Looking at the unicorn in these representations we are once again aware of contradictory images. From earliest days it had been connected with the idea of strength, virility, and even a certain arrogance. At the same time, however, it had often embodied gentleness and a desire for solitude. Now, as the unicorn becomes

gradually woven into the fabric of Christian allegory, we find it most frequently associated with virtue. Secular legends had suggested for some time that it could be captured by a virgin. Though pursued by hunters it would stop at the sight of a maiden and lay its head in her lap. It was natural, therefore, that with the cult of the Virgin Mary in the twelfth century the unicorn should be found with its head in her lap, and equally natural that it should come in time to serve as a symbol for Christ himself. Indeed, its very presence in a scene is now symbolic, as if people looking, for instance, at a tapestry would say to themselves, "Ah, yes, the unicorn is there," and feel reassured.

At the same time, however, as the unicorn became firmly established in the realm of allegory, "real" unicorns were in great demand. The horn had always had a reputation for possessing healing properties and for being able to detect poison. An illustration of this can be seen in the tapestry housed in The Cloisters, a part of the Metropolitan Museum of Art in New York City. Here we see a group of animals standing round while the uni-

corn dips its horn into a stream to purify it in order for them to drink. By the late sixteenth century unicorn horn was being greatly commercialized: fragments fetched high prices that only the rich could pay, and apothecaries ground it up to mix in potions as a cure for innumerable maladies ranging from scurvy and dropsy to fainting fits and melancholy. Some practitioners even invited prospective customers to view the horn itself, lest the authenticity of the medicine be in any doubt. Obviously these horns came from other animals: the single-horned Asian rhinoceros; the narwhal, or "sea unicorn," from the coastal waters of Greenland; even oxen and cows, pieces of whose horn were deceptively dyed. What is striking, though, is that for hundreds of years people believed so firmly in the existence of the unicorn and in the efficacy of its horn that such falsifications could be sold, not merely to the man in the street (who could barely afford them anyway) but to learned doctors and physicians, to kings and princes.

Gradually, of course, the unicorn found itself ever more firmly classified as a mythical creature, although,

like the Loch Ness monster, it is still sighted from time
to time. At the present, however, it seems to have
achieved a new burst of popularity. Ironically, fantasy has
a strong appeal in an age when science seems capable of
answering all our questions. We are, perhaps, tired of
certainties and feel uncomfortable in a world in which
there is a diminishing possibility of surprises. The contradictions in the unicorn have kept it alive for hundreds of
years, and artists are now turning to look at it in widely
diverging ways. Even as symbol it cannot be pinned
down. When we think we have tamed it, it escapes;
when we are ready to worship it, it turns into a devil.

25

26

Water flowers curve back their nighttime petals,
owls spread dreamwings in the starlight,
flamingos arch their gentle necks and dip their heads
to meet silver reflections in the stream.
The moon is spilling out of the sky in waterfalls of light;
a mist of scented jasmine hangs heavy in the air.
This is the night garden of the unicorn. Here he pastures
among drowsy ferns and humming insects,
caressed by spiderweb dreams, brushed
by the wings of midnight butterflies.

SS

In the heart of the forest a unicorn is born.
The trees hold gentle branches around it;
the forest pool guards its secret;
only the stars can see.
Among the silent spaces of the trees it grows
protected, nurtured by sunlight,
watched over by winds and soft-footed shadows.

36

I seek to come close to the unicorn,
to feel for myself the curve of its horn,
the cool of its satin silver skin.
In my dreams I caress it, possess it,
feel soft in my hair its dragonfly breath.
I roam with it in meadows high with flowers,
foxgloves, and daisies, the iris and the wild red rose.
The mountains rise blue and magical in the distance;
the sunlight sends golden needles
darting through the stream;
the air is heavy with the scent of lilies.
O unicorn, keep me by you!
Let me race with you to the far fringes
of the clouds; let me stand silent beside you
in pastures of snow.

11

The maiden is sent to seek out the unicorn.
Smooth and sudden as a flight of birds she enters
the maze of dappled shadow and he comes to her,
gentle as a rose, caught in her hair,
woven into the web of her mind,
multiplying softly within her.

49

*A*nd into the world came the unicorn: first and last;
flying on wings of milky glass, landing
like a satin ghost on the rocky promontories
of creation. It stands erect in the predawn wind,
waiting for earthrise. Around it blow silent winds,
while meteors and comets hurl their fire,
and dragon clouds collide.

The sky is as black as burnt paper.
Alien shapes in the night loom blind and foreboding;
hills, rocks and trees threaten with unfamiliar force
as I cower in the rising dark.
Manipulated by the forces of the night
the sea is a great black bubble,
swelling and flattening in a formless skin.
The moon makes no appearance
but, treading gently on the pathway of the
darkened rainbow, comes its emissary:
the unicorn. Points of light glisten in its mane
and in the flowing silk of its tail.

It shakes its head softly. Silver sparks rise in the void
like floating candles, drifting upward until they
fix themselves on the ceiling of the night sky.
I will reach up alone without fear into the night
and follow in the footsteps of the unicorn as it
moves along the dark arching road of the rainbow.
I will see the moon's secret face
and lose myself in the loneliness of the stars.
But within me the unicorn still remains,
a formless shadow in the spaces of my mind.
I stare at my reflection in the mirror.
Amber eyes hold me transfixed.
I press my forehead against the glass
and feel the flesh grow hard.

58

$\mathcal{U}$nicorn is a god.

He demands servitude and sacrifice.

He stands out of reach, as fixed and brilliant

as the stars. Serried ranks of unicorns keep guard

like anthracite statues on the outer edges

of our universe. Starlight catches on their horns,

their molded flanks glisten with power.

Hail, Unicorn! God of knowledge; a dark ghost

on the fringes of our consciousness,

a pewter shadow in the leafless deserts

of the mind.

The unicorn holds many secrets:
   the secrets of jungles and moonlight;
      the secrets that lie hidden at the roots of trees
         and conceal themselves in coral labyrinths
            beneath the ocean.
               I look deep into its amber eyes
                  and see my own reflection,
                     but altered in line and light,
                        as if in a dream.

he unicorn stands alone, still as frost.
  It keeps watch down corridors of time.
    The past and the future meet
      in the presence of the unicorn:
        the darkness and light become one.
        Patient as a candle flame,
            inviolate, here is our guardian,
              keeper of the silent unknown.

In my dreams the forest shrank back into its shadows,
the land faded behind me like a darkening mirage
and riding on the night ocean I saw a ship of glass.
With towers and curving staircases it rose
shining above the waves, driven by static winds
to the midnight edge of the world.
A silver unicorn stood at the helm.
His eyes glowed amber in the moonrise,
his mane blew out behind him
like threads of spun crystal.
In my dream I entered the vessel

and climbed to the top of the highest tower.
   The unicorn drove the boat across the waves
     and I knew that I was being carried
       at the heart of the universe.
        The waters shifted around me,
          the stars and planets spun themselves into oblivion;
           but here at the center all was fixed,
             supple as the raindrop,
               strong as the roots of the rose.

I saw the world in ruins. Temples fell,
trees were uprooted, mountains crumbled.
Great clouds of fire ate holes in the sky;
there was din and tumult and screaming.
Out of this cataclysm burst a unicorn,
riding across the heavens like a great war-horse.
It surged forward in a burst of gold:
its lips were parted, its eyes wild,
its great horn flashed like the dagger of a god.
This is the unicorn of the apocalypse,
the unicorn presence at the end of time.

t the world's edge, where earth and sky are one,
  where planets are sucked exploding into blackness
    and meteors with streaming tails
      whirl around in the motionless blast,
        a herd of unicorns plunges ecstatic and free;
        tails erect, manes streaming behind,
       horns and hooves outstretched
       like flying thunderbolts!

The unicorn is both dark and light.
It makes its home among the purple shadows of dusk;
it gallops ecstatic through the golden cornfields of noon.
It sees raging battles among the planets
and wanders at ease through meadows of silver cloud.
Its presence brings the brightness of lightning,
the power of the thunderbolt,
the softness of sudden summer rain.
It is at once creature of the morning
and beast of midnight.